Grow fruit

Gardening **organically**

One of the great joys of gardening is to experience the variety of life that a healthy garden contains. A garden managed using organic methods will have far more interest in it than a garden where insecticides and chemicals are used. An organic garden is a more balanced environment, where 'good' creatures such as ladybirds and beetles keep the 'bad' pests and diseases under control.

Organically grown plants also tend to be healthier and stronger than plants that rely on large doses of artificial fertiliser. In healthy soil they grow strong roots and can better withstand attack by pests and diseases. Soil can be kept in top condition by recycling garden waste to make nutritious compost. Growing the right combination of plants in the right place at the right time – by rotating where you plant your veg for example, or choosing shrubs to suit the growing conditions that your garden can offer – can deliver impressive disease-free results.

These are the basic principles of organic growing – use the natural resources you already have to create a balanced and vibrant garden. It's sustainable, cheaper than buying chemicals, easier than you think and great fun. Enjoy your organic gardening.

A warm, ripe raspberry freshly picked, the first strawberry of the year straight from the plant, the juicy crunch of a crisp, sweet apple in autumn from your own tree; these are some of the wonderful rewards for growing your own organic fruit – and it's fun to do!

Growing fruit may seem difficult at first but you don't need years of experience or lots of free time to succeed. This book should set you on your way and before you know it you will be hooked. It's not an expensive hobby and soon starts to repay your efforts with an organic harvest that others will envy.

Contents

1

The fruit you could soon be growing in your garden

Fruit grows on bushes, trees, canes and leafy plants. There is bound to be something that you can grow and enjoy in your garden, however small.

Choosing **what to grow**

Most fruit is best eaten straight from the plant. There is a strong chance that those warm ripe strawberries won't even make it to the kitchen. Fruit tends to be expensive to buy and can disappoint if not really fresh or ripe. Growing your own is not difficult provided you understand the basic principles.

First decide what fruits you particularly like. Then check the pages that follow to see what you can fit in your garden – this will save you from making a bad choice.

For more information look at the individual fruits in Chapter 4.

How soon can I expect fruit?

Strawberries can produce their first crop within 12 months. Autumn raspberries start with a small crop in their first year; other raspberries will fruit in their second year. Currants and gooseberries will also take a couple of years to start fruiting.

Tree fruit is slower to come into production; timing will depend on variety and rootstock. Apples, pears and plums will take 3 years.

Life expectancy

Apples, plums and pears can be very long-lived. Gooseberries, black and red currants may decline after 15 years or so; raspberries rarely stay healthy longer than 8 to12 years, depending on the soil; and strawberries are best replaced after 3 years. Obviously the better plants are cared for, the longer they will crop.

Local **climate** and **geography**

If your garden is in the north or high above sea level, the shorter growing season will restrict the varieties of apples and pears you can grow. Strawberries, raspberries and other soft fruits thrive throughout the UK; they just ripen a little later in cooler conditions. Plums blossom early, so their flowers are more likely to be killed by frost; which means no fruit.

A south or southwest facing wall absorbs heat from the sun, which then radiates back to provide extra warmth for trained fruit.

The west of the UK tends to be wetter than the east. Damp conditions in summer favour certain diseases, while other diseases thrive in the dry! Choose your varieties with the appropriate disease resistance.

Sunshine

In general the more sun the better the flavour, but you can grow redcurrants, gooseberries and cooking apples where there is some shade. Walls and fences facing south radiate warmth from the sun, useful for pears and plums; while apples grow best on southwest or west facing aspects. North-facing walls are good for redcurrants, gooseberries and some cooking apples. East-facing is not a good aspect, as rapid thawing from early morning sunshine can wither frosted blossoms, which might survive if they defrosted slowly.

Frost

Frost damages blossom, which means no fruit. Cold air settles into low-lying pockets of ground and gets trapped on the north side of walls, hedges and fences. You should be able to see where these pockets are in your garden by seeing where the frost thaws last, or not at all, on a sunny cold day. Avoid planting fruit varieties that flower early in these areas.

Wind

High winds lower the temperature, slowing growth, and blow away the flying insects that are needed to pollinate the flowers of most tree fruits. Some varieties of plum pollinate themselves, without the need for insects, and so will produce a crop in a windy site. However, for fruit to thrive, it is always preferable to provide some shelter, such as a hedge or fence. To be effective, a windbreak should be at least as high as the fruit you are growing.

Rain

Trees that are well established will usually manage on natural moisture levels in the soil. However young trees in their first three or four years and all other types of fruit, especially strawberries and raspberries, will need watering if the weather turns dry for more than two or three weeks.

Soil type and **acidity**

Apart from shallow soils over chalk, fruit can be grown on most soils types, as long as the drainage is reasonable. If other plants are thriving, then fruit should too.

You can improve a poor soil, but you cannot easily make a soil more acid. Most fruit prefer a slightly acid soil (pH around 6.5), though all but raspberries will tolerate moderately alkaline conditions.

If you think the soil may be too acid, or alkaline, test it with a home pH test kit. To make soil less acid, use dolomite limestone as instructed on the kit.

Space to grow

In Chapter 4 you will find advice on how much space to allow for each fruit type. You might be surprised at how much you can fit in, especially using trained forms – but don't overcrowd them.

Number of **varieties**

You will need to grow at least two different varieties of apple or pear, that flower at the same time, for pollination unless your neighbours are growing them too. Some plums varieties, and all soft fruits can pollinate themselves.

Ten good reasons to grow organic fruit

- The flavour of home-grown fruit is unbeatable

- You'll know they are grown without pesticides

- You can grow varieties that are not available in the shops

- You can pick it ripe and eat it fresh, unlike most bought fruit

- Kids will learn how fruits grow

- The whole family will benefit

- It's fun and can save you money

- It reconnects you with the seasons and seasonal eating

- Home harvested fruit is fresher than anything you can buy

- Your garden is as local as it gets

2

Fruit talk

Common fruit growing **terms**

Bud types: It is important to recognise bud types on fruit trees, so you don't prune out potential fruit. See 'Vegetative buds' and 'Fruit buds'.

Bush: The common simple shape for trees and shrubby fruits (except blackcurrants). A crown of evenly spaced branches arises from a single trunk or 'leg'. The centre is kept open by pruning to allow the sunshine and air in.

Cane: Raspberries grow as stiff stems from the ground, known as canes.

Cordon: A tree grown as a single branch usually planted at an angle of 45° to 60° to the vertical. Cordons can be trained upright on either side of an arch to meet; a series of these will make a tunnel. Cordons take up very little room, allowing several varieties to be grown in a small space.

Crown: Strawberry plants form a crown of fat buds from which grow leaves and fruits; also the upper branched part of a tree or bush.

Espalier: Trained form for apples and pears. Pairs of opposite branches are trained out horizontally from a central upright trunk in a flat plane.

Fan: Trained form for plums, redcurrants and gooseberries. Branches are spread out in a fan shape from a short trunk.

Feathered maiden: One-year-old tree with side shoots.

Fruit buds: A bud that will grow into a blossom and fruit; usually plump and rounded and pointing away from the branch.

Leader: The leading end shoot of a main branch or the whole main branch.

Maiden: A one-year-old tree.

One-year-old/two-year old wood: One-year-old wood is growth from the last growing season. This might still be in the same year in which you prune if you do it in November or December.

Organic: Grown to a recognised organic standard.

Pollination: Flowers need to be pollinated to produce fruit. Most soft fruits, and some tree fruits are 'self fertile', meaning they set fruit with their own pollen. Apples, pears and plums are generally not reliably self fertile, needing pollen from another variety of the same fruit. This is transferred by bees.

Resistant variety: Variety with in-bred or natural resistance to specific pests or diseases. This does not mean immunity!

Rootstock: Tree fruits usually consist of 2 parts, grafted together. The top part is the fruiting variety; bottom half (roots and stem) is the rootstock. Different rootstocks produce trees of different height and vigour and are given specific names. See p42.

Runner: Strawberries produce new plants on the end of long stems called runners.

Soft fruit: Strawberries, raspberries, currants and gooseberries.

Gooseberries, currants, raspberries and strawberries are known as soft fruit. Grow your own to experience real fruit flavour.

Spur: A side shoot from a main branch. Fruit buds usually form on these.

Stool: Old canes of raspberries and branches of blackcurrants, when cut back to the ground, form a stool.

Top fruit: Apples, pears and plums.

Trained forms: Many fruit plants can be trained, against a wall, fence or horizontal wires, in a variety of shapes.

Vegetative bud: A bud that will grow into a new shoot ; usually thin and pointed, lying flat to the branch or at a shoot.

Tips on preparing for healthy fruit plants

- Choose fruit that will thrive in your conditions

- Check what fruit grows well in neighbouring gardens

- Buy organically grown plants where possible

- Look for pest and disease resistant varieties to avoid trouble

- Keep fruit away from frost pockets and windy corners

- Avoid shady spots

- Check your soil acidity before planting

- Remember that you will need a new place to grow strawberries in three years time

- Put up supporting fences, wires etc before you plant so that you don't damage plants after planting

3

Getting started

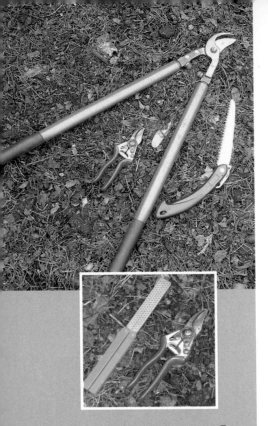

Tools

A spade, fork, hoe, rake, trowel, watering can, garden line and wheelbarrow form the basic toolset for the garden. For fruit growing you will also need some pruning tools: secateurs, loppers (for larger trees), a small pruning saw and a sharpening stone for the secateurs.

It is worth buying good quality tools, as they will last you longer and work better. Cheap secateurs, for example, are tiring to use.

Fruit pruning tools include secateurs, loppers (for larger trees), a small pruning saw and a sharpening stone.

Buying plants

Autumn planting is best so that plants are well rooted when leaves appear in spring. Plants are sold as 'bare-root' or 'pot-grown'. Bare-root plants are cheaper but should not be planted after March. Pot-grown plants can be planted at any time, but will need regular watering until established.

Organically grown top and soft fruit plants are now available. Specialist suppliers will offer the greatest choice of fruit. These will have mail order catalogues and, probably, an on-line ordering service. Look for the varieties with good flavour and resistance to pests and diseases. Don't buy more plants than you have room for.

Apple, pear and some plum trees need to be pollinated by another variety to produce fruit. Check in the catalogue that the varieties you choose will pollinate each other.

Top fruit comes on a choice of rootstocks (see page 42). Pick the one that best suits your garden.

As soon as your plants arrive, unpack them. Plant them immediately, or temporarily in an empty corner of the garden to stop the roots from drying out.

Choose a site

All fruit loves sunshine, so choose a spot that gets at least half the day's direct sunlight. Fruit does not like being crowded by other plants so ensure you have allowed enough space for the particular fruit (see individual fruits on pages 34 to 49).

Strawberries and raspberries are best grown in a row, so that they can easily be netted against birds. Currant and gooseberry bushes can be grown in their own bed or in a flower border. Redcurrants and gooseberries can also be grown in a line beside a path or against a fence or wall as cordons or fans. Blackcurrants can only be grown as bushes.

Apples, pears and plums can be planted as individual trees in a lawn or as cordons, fans and espaliers against a fence, wall or set of posts and wires.

Gooseberries and redcurrants can be grown as a cordon or fan, trained against wires or a wall. Redcurrants will even thrive against a north facing wall.

Preparing the ground

Fruit needs ground that is free from weeds, fertile and well cultivated to allow good drainage and easy rooting. If you are going to use land that was a flowerbed or a vegetable plot, all you will need to do is fork out any weeds and unwanted plants and add soil improvers, such as compost *(See Create Compost in the Green Essentials series – and, in this book, 'Feeding the soil' p. 27).*

Neglected **weedy ground**

The site may be very weedy or compacted. Since fruit does not like to grow in such conditions, it pays to put extra effort into preparing the ground and to prepare well in advance. (See *Grow Vegetables* in the *Green Essentials* series for further information on digging a plot).

As fruit is a long term crop, time taken to improve the soil and keep down competing weeds, (especially when young) will pay off.

Planting **into a lawn**

Top fruit can be planted into holes dug into a lawn or you may wish to make a bed alongside a path to grow cordons or other trained forms along wires or a fence. In either case the process is the same.

Step by **step** preparation

- Mark up the area with pegs or, if it is a round planting hole, score a circle in the turf with a sharp stick or spade.

- Slice off the turf about 2 to 3cm thick and stack it on one side. This will be good nutrient-rich material and you will use it later.

- Dig out the top spade's depth of soil.

- Loosen the next layer of soil with a fork.

- Put the turf in the bottom upside down and chop it up.

- Replace the top layer of soil.

Feeding the soil

Fruit lives for longer than vegetables, so it is important to get soil conditions right at the beginning. This will mean digging over as described above and 'feeding' the soil to make it more fertile before planting.

The best food for soil is compost, leafmould, manure or municipal compost mixed into the soil at planting time or

As a general rule use no more than one standard wheelbarrow full to every 10sq m of soil area.

spread on the surface subsequently. Details about the different types of soil food can be found in *Green Essentials, Grow Vegetables*.

Garden compost is the best soil food for fruit as it releases its nutrients slowly over several years, aiding growth when it is needed. As a general rule use no more than one standard wheelbarrow full (50kg approx) to every 10sq m of soil area. Too much plant food will cause excess leaf and wood growth at the expense of fruiting. Fortunately good home-made garden compost contains a balance of the nutrients that plants need. See *Create Compost* in the *Green Essentials* series for further information.

Planting

Once the soil is well prepared, you are ready to plant.

Strawberries

Buy for planting in early autumn or late spring. Plant 30 to 40cm apart in rows 75cm apart. Mark out the row. Using a trowel, scoop out planting holes large enough to take the spread-out roots of the plant easily, so that the crowns with the central boss of buds are just above soil level. Firm round the plant with your fingers or knuckles and water the plants in. You may wish to plant strawberries through a weed barrier which helps to protect the fruits later.

Raspberries

Plant in autumn. Plant 40cm apart in rows 1.5m apart, if you have space for more than one.

Raspberry plants are sold with a short length of old cane still attached. Plant up to the previous soil mark on this stub or a little deeper.

Loganberries are related to raspberries. Canes are long and need tying to wires.

Use a short stake to support fruit trees for the first few years. Trees on a very dwarfing rootstock, such as M27 and M9 for apples, will need a supporting stake for life.

Fruit **trees** and **bushes**

Dig out a hole large enough to take the roots easily and deep enough to ensure all the roots are below soil level.

Trees need a short stake to support them for the first few years unless they are trained to wires. Knock the stake into the ground, just off centre.

Put the plant in the hole and return some of the soil. Shake the plant gently to settle soil round the roots. Return the rest of the soil and adjust the plant in the hole so that it will be at the same planting depth as it was in the nursery. Note that blackcurrants should be planted 5cm deeper than the original soil mark, as this will encourage more growth from below ground.

Firm it in gently with your heel and rake the soil level around it.

Training and **support** systems

Raspberries and all trained forms of top and soft fruit need to be fixed to wires both to support them and to establish the shape.

To train trees to a wall you will need to fix upright lengths of batten to the wall every two metres to the full eventual width of the plant. For a fence this will not be necessary as you will be able to fix the wires to the fence posts.

For a free-standing support system you will need posts 2.4m long, 7.5cm thick either round or square – one for each end and another every 2m along the intervening row.

Fit wires at 45cm height intervals for trees and 30cm intervals for redcurrants and gooseberries, starting 60cm from soil level. For raspberries you will need just two wires, one at 135 to 140cm and one half way up the posts. Fix the top wire first, measuring and marking the positions carefully on the end posts.

To train trees to a wall you will need to fix upright lengths of batten to the wall every two metres to the full eventual width of the plant.

Tips on getting started with fruit

- Plant bare-root plants in autumn for best results

- Don't plant fruit where the same type of fruit has already been grown

- Prepare soil well before planting

- If soil is poor, allow a couple of years to improve it first
  (see *Grow Vegetables* in the *Green Essentials* series)

- Allow enough space for the fruit to grow to its full size

- Feed soil with garden compost matter for long-term fertility

- Do all the preparation, including putting up supports, before planting

- Don't plant too deeply or too shallowly

- Buy the best quality plants you can find for bumper crops to come

4

Fruits one by one

Strawberries

People associate strawberries with early summer but there are varieties to give fruit all the way to autumn. Plants tend to become very weak and diseased after 3 years; plant new crowns in a different place and remove the old ones.

To keep fruits clean and protected, tuck straw or weed barrier material under the leaves as fruits start to form. Remember to net your strawberries against birds!

After all the fruit is picked, cut off all the leaves and runners and put them on the compost heap with the straw. Leave a few centimetres of stalk to avoid cutting off the new buds.

Some common **strawberry** pests and diseases, and how to deal with them organically

Aphids – Squash by hand, encourage natural predators, spray with insecticidal soap.

Birds – Cover with netting.

Crown rot – Buy quality plants; never plant where strawberries have already been grown.

Spider mites – Keep plants watered in dry weather.

Grey mould – Never water the foliage; remove infected foliage and fruit promptly; use wider spacing, or keep plants only for one year where this disease is a regular problem.

Slugs – Pick off by hand; use traps; encourage natural predators.

Slugs are not a problem for most fruits, but they do love strawberries.

Raspberries

By growing a range of varieties - early, mid-season and late types, followed by autumn fruiters, you can harvest raspberries from June till November.

Plant canes 38-45cm apart, in rows 2m apart. They will grow to 2m or more in height and will need support,

For early, mid and late summer raspberries, you should cut the old wood (darker in colour) down to the ground at the end of the season. With autumn-fruiting plants you can cut all the canes down to the ground each year after fruiting has finished.

Some common **raspberry** pests and diseases, and how to deal with them organically

Aphids – Squash by hand; encourage natural predators; spray with insecticidal soap.

Birds – Cover with netting as fruit starts to ripen.

Raspberry beetle and cane midge – Remove mulches at end of season; take off netting to let birds get at the soil over winter; lightly fork over soil around canes in winter.

Cane spot, **cane blight and spur blight** – Check plants through the season for signs of these diseases, cut out and burn diseased canes.

To reduce potential damage from raspberry beetle, remove mulches at end of season, take off netting to allow birds to get at soil over winter and lightly fork around canes.

Gooseberries and **redcurrants**

Gooseberries are available as green or red fruited, for eating or cooking and currants and gooseberries freeze well.

Gooseberries and redcurrants can be available from June to early August if you grow several varieties. Your first small harvest will be two summers after planting.

Plant cordons 30 to 40cm apart and bushes 1.2 to 1.5m apart. To grow as a cordon buy a plant with a strong central leader; for bushes look for a plant two or three years old with 3 or 4 branches of equal size spread round the bush.

Pruning Cordons – Prune off side shoots to leave a clean 'leg' about 45cm high. Cut back the central leader by a third to a bud. Prune back remaining side shoots to leave three buds.

Pruning Bushes – Prune off any side growth to leave a 'leg' at least 40cm high. Keep 3 or 4 side shoots evenly spaced round the young bush and cut these back by half to a bud. Remove any others.

Common **redcurrant** and **gooseberry** pests and diseases – and how to deal with them organically

Aphids – Pick off infested leaves, or squash pests; encourage predators; spray with insecticidal soap.

Sawfly – Check plants for sawfly caterpillars from mid spring. Pick off by hand.

Birds – Particularly a problem for redcurrants. Net before fruit starts to ripen.

Mildew – Grow mildew resistant gooseberry varieties; prune out infected shoots and fruits; keep bushes pruned to allow good flow of air through the bush.

Aphids and sawfly are two common pests of gooseberries and currants. Regular checking will ensure you catch them early before they do much damage.

Blackcurrants

This fruit is stuffed full of Vitamin C and other goodness, especially when eaten fresh from the garden. You will be picking fruit two summers after you plant. Early varieties are harvested in June but July and August are the main months for the blackcurrant harvest.

Blackcurrants can only be grown as bushes and are quite large plants when fully grown. Allow 1.5 to 1.8m between each plant. Plant bushes about 5cm deeper than the soil mark on the stems. After fruiting cut back all the growth to leave just 2 buds above soil level on all the stems.

Some common **blackcurrant** pests and diseases, and how to deal with them organically

Aphids – Squash by hand; dislodge with a strong jet of water; encourage natural predators; spray with insecticidal soap.

Big bud mites – Cut out branches with swollen buds, which will be infected with the mite; grow resistant varieties.

Leaf-curling midge – Encourage natural predators; grow less susceptible varieties; remove mulches at the end of the season.

Mildew – Cut out diseased shoots; grow resistant varieties.

Ladybird adults and their larvae should be encouraged as they both feed voraciously on aphids.

Apples and pears

Although there are July cropping apples and pears, these fruits are principally of the autumn and winter. Late varieties are picked in autumn but have to be stored to ripen. Planting distances and final height vary according to the rootstock used. The most commonly used rootstocks are listed below. Some fruiting varieties are more vigorous than others, so heights will also vary with variety.

Apple rootstocks	Height	Planting distance
M27	1.5m to1.8m	1.2m to1.8m
M9	1.8m to 3m	2.5m to 3m
M26	2.4m to 4m	3m to 5m
MM106	4m to 5.5m	5.5m to 7m
Pear rootstocks		
QUINCE C	2.4m to 3m	3m to 4.5m
QUINCE A	3.6m to 4.5m	3.6m to 4.5m

Trees should not be allowed to carry a crop until the third summer after planting to allow them to establish a good root system. To prevent a crop developing early, pinch off any tiny fruits that appear in the first two years.

Some common **apple** and **pear** pests, and how to deal with them organically

Aphids – Squash by hand; dislodge with strong jet of water; encourage natural predators; spray with insecticidal soap. Scrub off woolly aphid clusters.

Sawfly – Pick up fallen fruit; replace mulches in winter.

Codling moth – Hang purchased codling moth traps in trees from mid-May to end July; attract Bluetits to the trees in winter.

Pear midge – Pick off small, deformed fruitlets; mulch under trees, replacing mulch each winter.

Apple and pear scab – Collect up fallen leaves in the winter, or run a mower over them so they decay quickly; cut out diseased twigs; grow resistant varieties.

Apple and pear mildew – Mulch under trees; water young trees in dry weather; cut out diseased shoots.

Apple and pear canker – Don't grow on waterlogged soil; cut out diseased branches; if a young plant is affected, it may be best to get rid of it.

Brown rot on apples – Prune out any diseased wood; remove all 'mummified' fruits left on the tree in winter; take away all windfall apples.

Pruning

Plants should be pruned after planting (before growth starts) and then annually in autumn to complete the forming of the desired shape.

Cordon – after planting, prune off any side growth from the trunk for the first 60cm from the ground. Cut back all other side shoots to 3 buds but leave the main leader unpruned.

In following years in late August, cut back the leader by a third of its new growth and continue working up the trunk reducing side shoots to 3 leaves. Spurs form from these. Prune back any new side shoots on these to one leaf.

Espalier - no branches must be allowed to form below the bottom wire. After planting, cut back the leader to a bud just above the bottom wire, allowing for a bud either side to be trained into the wires, or two side shoots, if they are well placed to line up with the wires.

Prune in winter to continue this process, gaining a level each year till you reach your top wire. Prune spurs as cordons.

Bush – look for 4 or 5 buds or 'feathers' spaced evenly round the trunk to make the main branches. Remove all others and cut back the central leader to just above the top feather. If there are no feathers, look for buds instead.

The following winter cut back all the new branches by a half to an outward-facing bud. In the next winter choose up to 6 of these, spaced evenly round the tree, to be permanent branches. Remove any others that originate from the trunk.

Winter pruning, when the tree is dormant, is used to encourage new fruiting wood and to shape the tree. Summer pruning, when the tree is in leaf, is used to restrict growth of trained forms.

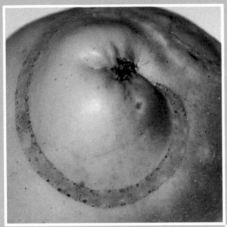

Sawfly damage. To minimise chances of attack, pick up fallen fruit; replace mulches in winter.

Brown rot. To help prevent spread, prune out any diseased wood; remove all 'mummified' fruits left on the tree in winter; remove windfall apples.

Summer pruning is used to improve the shape of trained varieties of apple.

Plums

Plums crop in late summer and autumn and cannot be stored for fresh fruit. Gages and damsons are also types of plum. The most useful rootstock for plums is 'Pixy', with a final height of 2.1m to 2.5m. Plant trees for training as a bush 2.5m to 3m apart; fan trained trees should be 5m apart.

Trees should not be allowed to carry a crop until the third summer after planting to allow them to establish a good root system. So pinch off any tiny fruits that appear in the first two years.

Plants should be pruned after planting (before growth starts) and then annually to complete the forming of the desired shape.

Bush – Cut back the central stem to leave 4 well-spaced 'feathers' to make the main branches. Cut off all others. If there are no feathers cut back to similarly placed buds.

To complete the forming of the shape, treat as for apples but prune in May.

Fan – The aim is to create a fan shape, with 6-8 evenly spaced arms either side of an open centre. Tie a bamboo cane into the supporting wires where you want each arm of the fan to grow – creating in effect a bamboo fan. A suitable shoot is tied into each cane.

Some common **plum** pests and diseases, and how to deal with them organically

Aphids – Check for this pest from mid winter on buds and twigs, then on leaves. Squash by hand; dislodge with strong jet of water; encourage natural predators; cut out badly infested shoots; spray with insecticidal soap.

Brown rot - Prune out all wilted blossom spurs and affected twigs. Pick up all fallen fruits, and remove every fruit from the tree.

Bacterial canker – Cut all branches that show signs of canker back to healthy wood as soon as possible; burn prunings.

Plum fruit moth – Hang up purchased plum moth traps in late spring; regularly pick up all fallen fruit.

Tips for successful crops

- Choose rootstocks of top fruits to suit the size of your garden

- Check that the varieties of apples, pears and plums you choose will pollinate each other

- Remove fruitlets on apples, pears and plums in their first two years

- Discard strawberry plants after three years

- Net strawberries, raspberries and redcurrants to keep birds away

- Prune new trees and bushes to establish their shape

- To get the angles you want for branches of fans, espaliers and cordons, tie canes to the wires and then tie the branches to the canes

- Tie new raspberry canes to the supporting wires as they grow

- Prune out old raspberry canes as soon as you have picked all the fruit

- To avoid pest and disease problems, never replant fruit in the same place

- Prune trained fruit in summer to keep growth in check

5

Looking after
your fruit

Keep an eye on things

Check over your fruit trees and bushes at least once a week during the growing season. By doing this you can spot problems early and deal with them. Simply picking off a pest, or a diseased leaf, early on can be all that is needed. It also helps you to learn what is likely to harm the plant and what can be ignored.

Some of the more common pests and diseases are listed on the specific fruit pages. You may need to consult a more detailed book to confirm your diagnosis before starting any treatment. You may also need to accept a certain amount of pest and disease damage, as there is not an easy answer to every problem.

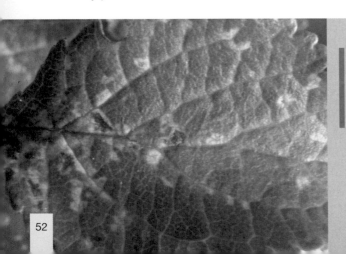

Plum rust - prune out diseased leaves and wood as soon you spot it.

Weeds

Weeds use up nutrients and water and need to be removed. Keep an area of at least one square metre in diameter free of weeds and grass around trees and bushes. Be careful of roots when you are hoeing or digging round plants. It is best to catch weeds when they are small. Regular weeding early in the year will soon reduce the problem. Use a hoe when the surface is dry but hand weed when the soil is moist.

Mulching is also effective against weeds.

Mulching

A mulch is any material applied thickly to cover the soil surface. Mulching stops weeds growing and conserves moisture in the soil. Usually mulches consist of natural substances such as straw, hay, leaves, green waste compost and rotted manure. Newspaper is also useful for bushes, trees and canes. Spread it 6 pages thick and cover in straw.

Always apply a mulch to a warm, wet soil. The ideal time for fruit mulching is in mid to late May.

Shallow rooting strawberries and raspberries benefit from a mulch to maintain soil moisture.

Water

Fruit contains a great deal of water, all of which the plant has to find from the soil. Strawberries and raspberries are particularly vulnerable to drought as their roots are near the surface.

You can do a lot to reduce the need for watering by preparing the soil well with compost (see p25) and by spreading a mulch on the surface. In hot dry weather you may need to water at least once a week .
A thorough soaking of 20 litres per square metre is better than regular small sprinklings, which soon evaporate.

The soil can be moist under a dry surface so, before watering, check the soil below the surface with your finger. Never waste water.

You can buy seep and drip watering systems that operate automatically and you should also use as many water butts as possible to catch and utilise rain.

Feeding

If you prepare the soil well, fruit will not need feeding in the first two years. After that you will need to give plants extra nutrients through the use of compost, manure through the use of compost and manure. These are all best applied in spring as plants start to grow. Fruits most likely to benefit from rich feeding - raspberries and blackcurrants.

It is possible to supply too much food, so you should only apply it when the plant shows signs of slowing growth. If, for example, a gooseberry bush grows less one summer than the previous year, it is a sign that you need to apply some compost the following spring.

Strawberries do not need heavy feeding. Spread leafmould (or compost on poor soils) just after you trim off the old leaves in summer.

Top tips for successful pruning

Pruning is an important part of keeping fruit healthy and promoting cropping. Some general tips are given below.

1   Always cut to just above a bud, side shoot or branch

2   Keep pruning tools clean and sharp

3   Do not prune in frosty weather

4   Learn the difference between a fruit bud and a vegetative bud (see p16)

5   Prune trained shapes (cordons, fans and espaliers) in summer – cutting in summer reduces vigour; winter pruning promotes new growth

6   Pruning is an opportunity to remove diseased tissue such as mildew and canker

7   Only prune plums between the middle of May and early September to avoid silverleaf disease

Annual pruning maintenance

Strawberries: Trim off all old foliage and runners after fruiting.

Raspberries – summer-fruiting: Cut out all old canes immediately after fruiting. Keep 10 healthy canes per metre of row and remove the rest.

Raspberries – autumn-fruiting: Cut all canes to the ground in winter. Do not prune in summer.

Redcurrants and **gooseberries**: Remove all growth from round the base. Keep the centre of bush forms open. In winter prune back leaders by about a third. Prune back all of this year's side growth to 2 or 3 buds. For cordons and fans in July reduce all side growth to 5 leaves of this year's growth, then to 2 or 3 buds in winter.

Blackcurrants: For simple pruning, in winter cut out all stems more than a year old to the ground to create a stool.

Blackcurrants before (above) and after pruning (below).

Apples and pears – bush: Keep the centre open. In winter start by pruning out diseased, dead and damaged wood. The tips of leaders often produce two or three shoots of equal length. Keep the middle one and remove any others. Prune out any strong vigorous upright growth back to where it starts and any side shoots growing from underneath a main branch. Leave all other spur systems till they are 4 years old, counting from the main branch, and then cut them back to where they started, leaving a very short stub.

Apples and pears – cordons and espaliers: Prune in late summer. Only prune shoots that are at least 20cm long. Cut back shoots arising directly from the centre leader or arms to 3 leaves. Cut back all side growth on the spur systems that develop to one leaf.

Cut back leaders by a third to a bud until they are long enough. Thereafter prune them back to a leaf of their new growth or a spur system.

As trees develop spurs can become crowded. Thin and shorten older spurs every winter by cutting out some of the twiggy growth.

Plums – bush: Plums should only be pruned between mid May and early September to avoid silverleaf disease. Bush plums need little pruning except to thin out dense, congested growth, dead and diseased tissue.

Plums – fans: Formative pruning is similar to a redcurrant fan. In late summer prune back all side shoots to 3 leaves.

Fruit **thinning**

Top fruits often set many more fruits than they can ripen and some plum varieties try to ripen far more fruits than the branches can bear. Some of these fall off naturally but it is better to reduce their numbers yourself, by hand. The aim is to thin the crop until there is about 15cm (6in) between each fruit, for apples and pears, and 10cm between plums. Keep the best-shaped, healthiest fruitlets and carefully remove the rest.

Prune cordon apples in mid to late summer to control vigour and get more fruit.

Top tips for healthy fruit

1. Choose varieties with natural resistance

2. Check plants regularly; pick off pests and prune out disease

3. Plant flowers nearby to attract hoverflies, lacewings and other creatures that eat pests (see *Green Essentials Grow Vegetables*)

4. Prepare soil well before planting; apply compost to keep soil healthy

5. Use sticky barriers and traps to catch pests

6. Don't replant strawberries with strawberries or raspberries

7. Prune fruit annually at the right time of year and don't let branches become congested

8. Thin fruits when they are small

9. Spray the leaves with liquid seaweed every few weeks from spring to fruit set

10. Make sure you know a friend from an enemy when checking for pests

11. If you do need to use a pest spray, choose one designed for an organic garden

See *Grow Vegetables* and *Control Pests* in the *Green Essentials* series for further information.

Codling moths, an apple pest, can be caught in a sticky trap, baited with a pheromone.

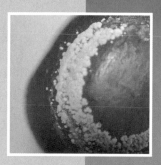

Apple brown rot is a common disease of apples. Pick up all fallen fruits, and remove any 'mummified' fruits remaining on the tree.

Apple canker - cut out diseased branches immediately

Want more organic gardening help?

Then join HDRA, the national charity for organic gardening, farming and food.

As a member of HDRA you'll gain-
- free access to our Gardening Advisory Service
- access to our three gardens in Warwickshire, Kent and Essex and to 10 more gardens around the UK
- opportunities to attend courses and talks or visit other gardens on Organic Gardens Open Weekends
- discounts when ordering from the Organic Gardening Catalogue
- discounted membership of the Heritage Seed Library
- quarterly magazines full of useful information

You'll also be supporting-
- the conservation of heritage seeds
- an overseas organic advisory service to help small-scale farmers in the tropics
- Duchy Originals HDRA Organic Gardens for Schools
- HDRA Organic Food For All campaign
- research into organic agriculture

To join HDRA ring: **024 7630 3517**
email: **enquiries@hdra.org.uk**
or visit our website: **www.hdra.org.uk**

Charity No. 298104

Resources

HDRA the organic organisation promoting organic gardening farming and food
www.hdra.org.uk
024 7630 3517

The HDRA Encyclopedia of Organic Gardening
Dorling Kindersley
editor Pauline Pears

Soil Association the heart of organic food and farming
www.soilassociation.org
0117 929 0661

MAIL ORDER:

The Organic Gardening Catalogue
Organic seeds, composts, raised beds, barriers, traps and other organic gardening sundries. All purchases help to fund the HDRA's charity work.
www.organiccatalogue.com
0845 1301304

Buckingham Nurseries
– fruit trees and bushes
www.buckingham-nurseries.co.uk
01280 822133

Butterworth's Organic Nursery –
organic fruit trees
www.butterworthsorganicnursery.co.uk
01290 551088

Harrod Horticultural
www.harrodhorticultural.com
01502 505300

Tamar Organics – organic fruit trees
www.tamarorganics.co.uk
01822 834887

Walcot Organic Nursery
– organic fruit trees and bushes
www.walcotnursery.co.uk
01386 553697

Welsh Fruit Stocks – organic soft fruit
www.welshfruitstocks.co.uk
01497 851209

who, what, where, when and why organic?

for all the answers and tempting offers go to www.whyorganic.org

- Mouthwatering offers on organic produce
- Organic places to shop and stay across the UK
- Seasonal recipes from celebrity chefs
- Expert advice on your food and health
- Soil Association food club – join for just £1 a month

Soil Association
the heart of organic food & farming